For Yvonne, 8th Sept 2010

with much love

from

Julie ~ Bruce.

Collusions

Collusions

Julia Wroughton *Drawings*
Bruce Killeen *Poems*

STRATHMORE PUBLISHING

LONDON

2010

First published in Great Britain by Strathmore Publishing,
41 Kingsway Place, Sans Walk, London EC1R 0LU, 2010

ISBN 978-0-9550887-7-3

Previously published by the same authors

Evocations
Wood Engravings and Poems
2007

Digressions
Drawings and Poems
2008

Design and origination by David McLean, London
Typeset in Sabon, a typeface designed by Jan Tschichold
Printed in England by Portland Print, Kettering, Northants, NN16 8UN

Foreword

The drawings came first. The poems are a personal response to them. They are not intended to be illustrations, that would be redundant.

Are they poems? Or stories? Or character-sketches? Perhaps *Collusions* asks these questions more than our earlier books. Academic definitions requiring a writer to work within a specific discipline seem to me to limit creativity. I like to break boundaries and jump frontiers. I like to think that the drawings and poems collide or collude to create a third, imagined art form.

Neither the rather slight sketches nor the more developed drawings claim profundity but they are observed, concerned with the visible world: they resist the explanatory, they make their effect slowly.

The poems come from looking through sketchbooks and drawing books – a pleasurable and enlarging experience. And I want to pass on something of that. They are designed to be read aloud.

B. K.

Contents

Foreword   5

Tailor-Made   8

A Country Afternoon   10

What do Flowers Contribute?   12

A Castle in the South   14

The Scholar   18

The Demonstration   20

Chair, *Morning Light*   22

The Tumble of the Wind   24

Absentee   26

To the Hilt   28

Rain in Venice   30

On Silent Castors   32

Her Own Island   34

A Frail White Thread   36

A Farm in the Gers   38

New Shapes of Light   40

A Moment's Life   42

He Knows his Mind   46

Breaking Free   48

McKinnon's Cave   52

Time to Go   54

Winter Light   56

Typewriters   58

That Wild Track   62

Generosity of Intent   64

Escape Route   66

Acceptance   68

All the Bells are ringing   70

Music Patron   72

Chair, *Evening Light*   76

Afterword   79

Biographcal note   80

Tailor-Made

Protecting not from cold but from heat
these darkened shadows, tailor-made,
fit them like another coat
repeat the rounded forms of sheep.

In this most northern part
of silver-sand Iona
a coolness with the silence should prevail
but this year, the summer sun determined
reached every bank and sandune
all those concavities
re-shaped by wind and rain.

The wind has dropped at last
a boat anchored in the bay
a tall girl stands calmly on the deck
is diving in, is swimming now.
For sheep, all activity is over:
they do not need to move.

A Country Afternoon

Andrew had his feet up
when we came
the shameful grass
too long to cut
and the midges
went for Michael
more tasty than the tree
and Julie dropped the tray
and burnt the poet's foot;
disaster was the order of the day
and all this because
the furniture
looked like Andrew anyway
not ugly, not at all,
but strong and made of iron.

What do Flowers Contribute?

The light is savage
and is soft,
melting and precise,
approximate, exact.
What authority
the flowers impose.
How tentative the figure,
a panelled door half open,
slot of mirror overhead,
these triumphs of transition.

In this passage
in this room
what do flowers contribute?
A focus,
a cleansing,
an announcement.
Even behind front doors
the smallest flower can dominate,
assert its own brief life.

A Castle in the South

Sometime the sun will pause
flatten knock down walls
re-build them further off,
space pulled out
binoculared at will.

Across the vast plain below
verticals grow taller
long shadows lengthen.

Backs of houses
scattered barns,
escarpments, outcrops, rows of trees
stand up, demand a recognition.

Tomorrow every shadow gone
detail lost in generality.
Amongst those smudgy forms
so clear before
only the castle on the hill
the massive battlemented tower
asserts a dark authority.
The darkest part of all the door,
retaining hinges still intact
where does that lead,
backwards, sideways
through six centuries
of triumph and dismay?
Upon what nursery story
what children's yarn
does this depend?

Dustproof, brilliantly preserved
wardrobe of ancient costumes;
an admiral's uniform complete,
silver coins wrapped-up in manuscripts
in little leather pouches
and everywhere on every floor
from state rooms to the cellarage
(or are they dungeons after all?)
heavy magazines are strewn about
or neatly tied in bundles;
did no one cancel a subscription
no one stop the flow?

But again
a change of light,
new sun makes nonsense
of it all.
The tower has lightened,
a pinkish grey on palest blue
a ghost of former self
a breeze could blow it all away
insubstantial with its treasure;
a part of history gone,
a needed memory,
a noble gesture never made.

The Scholar

Where hands find warmth
eyelids droop
words stay on the page
too comfortable by half.

Calm between footnotes
Scylla and Charybdis well astern
not a mark too big
a scratch too small
not a nail-pairing out of place
the cold thrill of reproof,
a text amended
a provenance proclaimed
re-established beyond all doubt;
with diligence you keep in check
those flames that cannot burn.

But doubt is all the poet knows,
a lifting of the lip
alembic for a truth but half-perceived.

Sir poet dormant,
how can you write so, sitting down
too comfortable by half,
re-shape the gesture to the content,
the fervour, the fervour of it now.

Go my little writing pad
into that fiery furnace
let words to ashes burn
save only foot-notes
let feeling not return.

The Demonstration

It swept through the cathedral
like the Atlantic
triforium high,
west window to baldachino.

I watched dear Simon from behind.
He seemed above it all,
out of touch,
ten miles away.

This total grand immersion,
an organ either end
the stops near fully out,
the scraps of light on capitals
the shadows in the vaulting
so intimate, so ultimately contained,
virtuoso demonstration...
but where's the music gone?

When the flood subsided
we went out slowly, stricken,
through a narrow corner
of the great west door
to the sudden light
and Simon said,
Interesting the sounds of traffic
never thought of that before.

Chair
Morning Light

The morning light comes first
until the trees begin their dance:
the curtain darkens lifts a little,
the white and painted shutter
acquires a warmer sheen.
Abruptly the sun,
a stranger at the door
demands an instant entrance.
The morning light
has forced its way
finds the chair at once
proclaims its brief authority.

The Tumble of the Wind

Can a few words
that break a stanza-line,
flimsy scribble
with a fibre pen
make manifest a mountain,
the tumble of the wind?

The pantheist
loved relationships
mood-swopping,
identity parades.
When I look at a Constable
the Swiss Fuseli said,
I call for my greatcoat
and my umbrella.

The magnanimity of the mountain
bad temper of the wind
I felt it out there then
I feel it all within
right across the notebook page
four inches of a fibre pen.

Absentee

The little chair
along the wall
who placed it there
and why?

The way ahead
that veering to the left,
re-allocates the landscape
re-makes pasture, meadow,
hillside, forest;
imposes stricter geometry.

Recover breath
make most of this:
the wall that draws the world
will scarcely mark a track
no traveller to record;
the chair be but illusion
the absentee imagined –
walls were deceivers ever.

To the Hilt

An essay in concentration:
disappearing of the neck,
a slight leaning forward,
controlled angle of attack:
a deep-end diving in,
no withholding back.

Agnew McMaster
a slogan for his cast,
... to-the-hilt, the very hilt,
from Galloway the words still echo.

But this is rubbish in a shed
why tó-the-hilt for that?
When a new old house is round the corner
why aren't you drawing there?

The grand front doors are open
the sun has made its mark
danced on fruit and bathroom tap,
there's plenty there to draw
or write about for that.

Out there in the timeless shed
form from function separated
in ambiguity of light and shadow
bits and pieces re-assemble
make richer, unanticipated shapes
new images to master.
Nostalgia, sentiment play little part;
in this partnership, this transformation.

Rain in Venice

Under the inadequate canopy
(not meant for heavy showers)
the last tourists wait
blurred images upside down –
the broken mirrors of the rain.

Walls melt into sky
the sky another wall.

In the church a painted sky
saints and angels take advantage
sharp-winged and dark as bats or birds
no doubts or softened edge
their space is infinite
their time for ever
their confidence absolute.

The plastic chairs
are taken in
the lady on the step
has shut the door
more tourists come
too much for her.

The sun renewed
they march in twos
and fours
dive in and out,
the darkness of the church
sparkling light outside
their confidence is absolute.

On Silent Castors

Its not everyday
it rains like this
but most days, the days
are not the same
measure them if you can:
this monotony of greys.
The rain will move the headlands
backwards, forwards on silent castors,
or rub them out entirely.

Clouds reform
reclaim a shape
their deep echo
comes and goes,
oncoming cessation
of wind, of rain.

Cold light on rockface
flashes back its message
tilted field
abandoned boathouse
broken stone
come alight, go out.

The contours right in front
acquire a vicious look
skylines blacken, headlands menace
– continuous theatrical performance
along this monotony of coast.
Do we have them once again?
We do, but it is different all the same.

Her Own Island

Tall and wealthy
affable and concerned:
A world tour, he asked?
Why not; she did a thing she rarely did –
a straight look at amber eyes
bounced back reflection
found a softness deep within,
potentiality for forgiveness.
He had climbed so far so fast:
come with me
those brown eyes said
not cat and mouse
she didn't want to hear.

He planned it all
something he had to do
they paused at last
a place to talk
We've done it all before John
and so they had and hadn't
the glass she never emptied
the far off absent look.
Fair hair lifting on a sudden wind

And who is that behind,
the tall girl with the easel
here before we came:
in the still centre
of the world's turning
she makes her own island
an inch beyond approach.

You've shown me half the planet John
lets stay at home next time
I see you clearly now –
no chain and bridle, no
he planned it all –
(India, South America,
bits of Europe, even)
each place a tale to tell.

The lies of all
the colour brochures
make much more sense to me.

A Frail White Thread

From mountain-top
to wide sea-edge
the river's not difficult to follow,
sometimes a narrow thread,
(a strand of cotton on a shadowed floor)
sometimes wide enough to spread
along the cliff, white sky and water merging.

Soon it disappears behind the road
becomes much broader, visible again,
a meandering harmless sort of river,
makes an ox-bow for the farmer-
a place to wash his dogs in so he says.

Then new energy is found,
it charges at the watergate
lifts the lighter boards,
plays them like piano keys
they rise and fall,
catch light, go dark
the smaller stones dispersed,
it pours down blackened boulders,
old men's silver hair.

Beneath another road, a narrow bridge too small
the river forces through its way,
its prettiness replaced by menace now,
finds flat and boggy ground,
breaks banks, diverts, circumnavigates,
resumes the mainstream onward flow,
and then, inexplicably, it stops…
beyond the ledge flows far below.

Can a frail white thread
from another world change identity
as a person can,
change scale if not intention?

It is not the size
of this great fall,
the drama or the gesture,
but the constancy that intimidates,
a thousand years indifference,
a thousand years to come.

A Farm in the Gers

Nothing shouts here
except perhaps the pigeonnier
charming yes, but drives
an assertive wedge;
makes its presence felt,
everyone must stay in rank
retain a humble place.

Light goes, the farm darkens
spreads like a tabby cat
then stripes subdue, buildings merge
blend of dark with dark
only the pigeonnier pyramid
maintains a softened dominance.

In England it is towers
and rounded barns –
agreeable to cumulous,
awkward on clear sky.
Here the triangle has its way.

Why this desperate yearning
for a dull and better world,
the absurdity of harmony?
(Rafael's assonance created
in a time of strife;
the placing of a circle
above a doorway at San Miniato –
whose music that?)

Natural or man-made
the sound of birds, or symphonies –
its universe moves in harmony
(the silent music of the spheres)
why not this particular place –
the silence of the farmyard here?

And why as I walk along
these lonely roads in Gascony
and study sky lines and dream of harmonies
do I feel a kind of guilt?

New Shapes of Light

These two chairs
and the white-backed one
on the right
tell me who was here
and what they said and why,
not that I really want to know.

This small kitchen
the implication of activity
the chair that's left askew,
the fruit-bowl so neglected
(the last apple might be taken,
the teapot should be filled)
industry never ceases,
fridge audibly joining in,
the clock an hour behind
but what of that?
There's nothing that does not happen here.

Today is Monday.
The sky is blue.
Two jets fly overhead.
Is their scream a taking-part?
They leave no mark.
Sky less perfect than it was.
Inside and outside
new shapes of light are made,
tall panels slide along the wall,
bowl and jar extend new shadows,
vast distances between.

As laddered light
extends across the ceiling
objects change as people do
(who can testify his own identity?)
The room encaged opens gates again
the antipodes are close at hand.
From this much used and casual kitchen
my Pacific Ocean's made,
my own small peak in Darien.

A Moment's Life

The door closed with a bang.
I'd gone to sleep I think.
The Sotto Portego is my dream.
Far off, two figures meet
talk a moment, part and meet again –
an afterthought, a date to fix.
Bright light behind, comes forward,
silhouettes their shape, withdraws,
there's nothing there
there never was
an empty stage
footlights but no figures.

The man with the stick,
a carrier bag
(the small dog's from somewhere else I think)
he's further off,
another plane,
a previous, perhaps forthcoming scene.

In the foreground those sturdy guardsmen
turned to stone,
when did they appear,
who put them there?
but they haven't settled yet,
restlessly they play their part.

Those scenes so sharply sub-divided,
those memories
that shunt about like little trucks
that telescoping, tunnelled vision
gives animation, a moment's life
or puts them back to sleep again –
the Sotto Portego of my dream.

He Knows his Mind

A destination, what is that?
Something to discover,
the end of ceaseless search?

Better for the tree
rooted on the spot
to grow with leaps and bounds
(the joy of the ascent
collide, too rough a concept,)
embrace could be appropriate
but by sudden whim or chance,
nothing is by planning
by malevolence or plot.

The power within the limb
the discovery of this,
the movement in rehearsal
repeated gesture,
echo down the line,
a gregarious or a private celebration.
Is the best dance of all,
the one that's danced alone?
Man and dog
move quietly
through the scene
they share a rather apprehensive
kind of peace

the destination for the man
is far from clear
and that little dog
so hastily redrawn
why does he seem so stupid?
Because he knows his mind?

Breaking Free

Jane

She makes her own decisions
quietly, unobserved…
She stayed at home a week
(a day or two at any rate)

Imposed upon, she thought
that picture should be straight
(the lopsided family group)
we live within its frame –
proximity for survival
but I'm a breaker – out,
just on parole, I guess?
David saw to that.

Pert little thing, he called me,
interfering hussy once:
that little saved his bacon then,
A little term of endearment
he would have said.
Do I smile dear, do I cringe?

David swimming, so masculine, ridiculous
the hail and farewell of waving arms;
the getting dry, reflecting sand
his white towel on a dark sea
angels wings I thought –
I nearly fell for that.

She stood up suddenly
jersey pulled right down,
pleated skirt an after-thought
challenging or disregarded.

I see him clearly now
his teasing provocation
a toreador in the ring –
white towel or angels wings?
black cloak of death more like.

Let me straighten the picture,
renew the frame
quietly, unobserved:
God gave me eyes,
I know a right-angle
When I see one

McKinnon's Cave

Do we assume McKinnon was a man of peace?
a contemplative from the start?
It was a brave thing to do
to cross those northern seas to far Iona –
long time before the Vikings came.

Were the brethren more than he could stand?
(theirs was not a silent Order) –
the refectory he had helped to build,
the eating and the coughing,
the breaking of the stones,
the scriptorium an only solace.

Cloudless days, the clarity of light,
the melancholy of silver sand,
emerald green of sheltered bays,
it was a brave thing to do
to seek another place.

At Staffa the cliffs are so much higher,
the rocks and boulders twice as steep
and day and night, relentless;
like the sound of distant cannon
the pounding of the sea.
McKinnon came to know the island well
almost to accept the noise and fury,
it was a brave thing to do
to seek another place.

But the Isle of Mull he found at last,
a stillness and a kind of peace,
found the tumbled confusion of the rock
poised, balanced, split in two
been there a million years
could have fallen yesterday.

At the entrance to a tunnel
where jets of water turn to spray
white goats took shelter either side
beyond them the darkness of a double-cave…
It was a brave thing to do to live the life he wanted there,
a man of peace,
a contemplative from the start.

Time to Go

As the sun moves
so shadows move
swiftly, silently
they stripe the path,
make stripes on passers-by.

Definitions made ambiguous
blurred forms across
the valley lost,
suddenly it is time to go.

The house, the steps
the statuary
the hero and the flautist
the palm tree
shrouded unassailable
lost identities…

The struggle to be noticed
to make a mark to be successful
achieve respect,
suddenly it is time to go.

Winter Light

Those long debated skies
the possibility of this and that
the battlemented clouds
or emigrating sheep
the tumult and the drama

Bright light obliterates

This wild piece of ground
broken gate, depleted hedge
unwanted sea behind
were they ever there
ever there at all?

Bright light obliterates

The dark, stricken oak
not yet ready for oblivion
makes a last demonstration
of an ancient, final strength

Bright light obliterates

Typewriters

Ridiculous in your small room, my friend said –
A cinema organ rising, sinking,
The Gaumont, Odeon, Hippodrome
(Sandy MacPhearson, you know).

He was a big fellow certainly
friend of many years
a masculine sort of person,
made me toe the party-line
didn't like a split infinitive
forced me often into rhyme
sometimes we got on pretty well –
my first dear typewriter and I
just once or twice I pulled out all the stops
the magic of that sharing was sublime.

Now, this delightful little green person
(colour of a field in Westmorland
only after rain of course).
You served me well without complaint
although your 'a's are inclined to stick.
(Your question mark needs a Hercules
to show at all but I'm not one to interrogate);
just as inspiration is warming up
all your keys will sometimes jam.

Between the devious lines and paper
what hazards are in store?
What tiny triumphs, what bleak despairs, are in store
circumlocution, avoidance of the point,
my first thoughts are never black and white,
oyster-catchers taking off,
they start by overlapping
but later change to grey.
First and last thoughts never synchronize;
old truths refocus, insistently come back.

O my little green friend
you have found out so much, so much;
how to give confidence to the tentative
finality to all my listless wandering
and if I sometimes loose
a word, a line,
yours is not the voice that says –
The number you have dialled
has not been recognised.

61

That Wild Track

There are gates
that want to be opened,
gates that demand to be shut,
come-hither gates
and keep-your-distance gates.

Frail trees
scratch sudden mountains
rocks obdurate
aggressive edges
unassailable.

So go thy ways stranger
that wild track of land is not for you,
draw your curtains closely
go home and put the kettle on.

Generosity of Intent

Single stalks of corn made sheaves
(fifty years ago)
Rods of rain, a shower
(its thus to day)
pencilled marks assembled,
a small army on the move,
order, direction, purpose,
they open-up, advance,
any error could be disastrous
they march together or not at all.

A group of lines assiduously maintained
find their own free way
of folding over land,
new subject matter rapidly aligned.

On the right the yielding trees
the wild ascending hedges,
shorter scrub along the top,
surprising for the climb.

No detail admitted from the start
nor any impediment to the spread,
the broadness of the drawing absolute
condition a generosity of intent.

Escape Route

The New York painters came here
to break the pressure from their work,
meet the challenge of the sea,
the artist's inner torment,
ability for extravert delight.

The immensity of this prospect
the wind in waving grass,
huge blocks of granite
that keep the sands in place,
bright light on weathered board,
those bathtubs that make mockery
of modern plastic boats.
Cape Cod inspires, re-forms,
cleanses the complex mind
brings back directness,
an ultimate simplicity –
the exhilaration of relief;
sends back to New York City
those proud desperadoes of the chase.

Acceptance

Feats of strength or frailty;
Egyptians, Babylonians, Berliners
built their walls
for the same purpose
made fast a piece of land
to keep within, without;
hostile, preventative;
these are the world's dividers,
keep man from desperate man.

This untroubled fence though,
how lightly it makes its way
follows the tumble of the wall
sunlit spaces in between
inviting or denying,
every stake eccentric
in its own particular way
responsive to every weather;
a mocking fence,
a ruin of a wall,
maybe last for ever.

Tread warily the splintered wood
bits of wire, broken stakes
there's no new territory to claim:
kill curiosity, ambition, greed,
(the adventure of the mouse)
accept the strength of this fragility.

All the Bells are Ringing

The pedestrian placards his disbelief
he tightens coat, quickens pace
branches lift with like indifference:
they are not moved by this irrelevance,
the bells of Gesuati toll in vain
a big city makes big demands.
We can all be rational for a little while, a little while
and then the emptiness, the darkness or the void.

Two thousand years of con-trick to be sure,
may be ten thousand years of need:
then fill the gap and tell me
why all the bells are ringing…
I don't care who makes them go,
men, machines, or little boys –
the sound is universal, universally understood.

The Tiepolo extends its harmony,
his grand staircase to a multi-coloured heaven,
the unbeliever holds his breath –
all the bells are ringing,
a new Pope has been elected –
the strength of continuity.

All the bells are ringing!

Music Patron

Fauré and Chausson
could have been her friends
long dead but so alive
and Madame de Clairmont
the Muse of Malplaquet
they call her now,
she'll take a bit of stopping
I know her staying power.
Something could be done.

So why do I have doubts,
Wineretta so long gone?
I could organize the concerts
do committee work
(as far as I could stand it).
Somewhere near the Pyrenees
cherry blossom all along –
deep-blue mountain overhead.
Casals was down there once:
what a place to start a Festival.
I could keep my own playing going too,
that's important is it not?
Something could be done.

The Guildhall players wouldn't charge
(expenses only to begin with
but that's not good enough).
Would father's fortune go so far?
Michael is a fund-raiser

and that's where we begin.
My provenance is sufficient,
beloved, hateful New York City
the traffic like sweet lavender
the opera at the Met.,
the warmth, applause… applause?
Is that all I really want?

All you want is power Paul said
this Festival of yours is phoney.
Dear brother, you are not my keeper, no
If the village take it well,
if it is a friendly place,
If France is what I think it be
then banners, flags, oriflammes will fly.
Don't worry, Paul dear boy
my celebration will be muted
you know why
something could be done.

I'll bring it off, you'll see
Fauré, Chausson, those that follow in their wake
are life and death to me,
my life right now,
my life to come.

Chair
Evening Light

Time insists on knowing things,
moves sideways as well as back –
Who sat on this chair and why?
Who owns the clock behind?
Where are they now?
Laughing, talking, dreaming –
another life, another place;
freed from the chair
freed from the clock
do they become a different person
the chair a different chair?

Left on its own,
at first we see another person
sitting there.

Shadows wrap in secret
this secret place:
outlines gently slip away,
last light touches cushion,
slides down concave arm:
the furniture closes up
the room grows smaller
walls fast-fading, disappear.

But this is a grand armchair
worthy of substantial man
repose, command, the will to win

a chair to dominate,
bring a conference to conclusion.

It has its place,
acquires the character
of those who use it
or gives back, becomes itself.
Here in this setting
we know who seeks its peace
who was happy here,
who found rest.

Afterword
For R.P. who found the poems melancholy

I'm sorry you think
they're melancholy –
I'd like you
to feel their joy
(there is joy
is there not?)
I meant it so.

Where waves break
gulls scatter,
two whites together;
torn paper
in laconic wind:
that is joy
– yes or no?

Two whites together,
that'll change the world!
(the vitality
of triviality)
wars will cease
and kissing come;
God-given is my joy.

Julia Wroughton studied at Colchester School of Art and the Royal College of Art in London. She taught in several Art Schools and later founded Inniemore School of Painting on the Isle of Mull where she still lives and paints. She has exhibited frequently in London, Bristol and Edinburgh and has paintings in private and public collections in Britain and abroad.

Bruce Killeen has exhibited at the Royal Academy and the Royal West of England Academy and he has had Solo exhibitions with the Artists' International Association and the Drian Galleries in London and more recently at galleries in Edinburgh. He was a tutor at the Royal Academy Schools and an Art Correspondent for the Guardian. He now works on the Isle of Mull.